2016–2017

THE ENGAGED CITIZEN

A Selection of
Student Writing for
the University of
Kentucky's Department
of Writing, Rhetoric,
and Digital Studies

VAN-GRINER

The Engaged Citizen

A Selection of Student Writing for the University of Kentucky's
Department of Writing, Rhetoric, and Digital Studies
University of Kentucky
2016–2017

Printed in the United States of America
10 9 8 7 6 5 4 3 2 1
ISBN: 978-1-61740-405-4

Van-Griner Publishing
Cincinnati, Ohio
www.van-griner.com

CEO: Mike Griner
President: Dreis Van Landuyt
Project Manager: Maria Walterbusch
Customer Care Lead: Julie Reichert

Kirkman 405-4 Su16
173805
Copyright © 2017

Table of Contents

Individual Projects

Group Projects

The digital projects all include a QR Code that will take you to the project online. If you don't have a QR reader, you can go to our website (https://wrd.as.uky.edu) and click on Composition and Communication.

Knocking Out Parkinson's

Melanie Berexa

For the WRD 110 documentaries on difference, students are often drawn to communities such as the autistic population, the homeless community, or Alzheimer's patients and caretakers. These are such important topics, but very broad, and students puzzle over how to fit an entire complex group of people into a five-minute documentary. One of the challenges of the documentary project is finding a way to tell a story that connects the audience with these huge issues in a poignant way; the temptation is to instead make a purely informational video that lists facts about the community, but doesn't draw us into a narrative. These videos are not *bad,* but they don't inspire the audience to act in the way a good story does.

Melanie soared over this common pitfall. She created a documentary with a clear narrative arc that is also firmly contextualized with necessary information and research. By highlighting one person's journey, she makes the audience invested in the broader topic. She uses captivating interviews and upbeat music to tell Dr. Mike Bell's story in a way that is respectful, fascinating, and thoroughly inspiring.

—Anna Stone

Scan the QR code to see the project online.

Dialectically Different

Cassidy Breeding

The first word that comes to mind when I think of Cassidy's documentary is *beauty.* Of course I'm thinking of the seamless editing, gorgeous videography, and careful organization, but I'm also thinking of the love and appreciation with which Cassidy constructs this narrative. The assignment for our WRD 110 class was to create a documentary that highlights a community of difference; she tells her story of difference with passion, grace, and dignity. The result is a powerful piece which highlights the beauty of Appalachian speech and culture.

—Anna Stone

Scan the QR code to see the project online.

Brothers in Number Seven

Kayla Burton

Kayla's piece is a remarkably pure bit of cinéma vérité about two elderly brothers who have a close relationship, at once nearly symbiotic and yet affectionately combative. These sorts of portraits demand a mastery of tone—you don't want to be exploitive, but there's also the risk of being way too touchy feely fuzzy wuzzy. Using a completely observational approach—no voice over, nondiegetic music, or overt emotional cues—she paints a poignant, amusing, genuinely quirky picture of two brothers who are both family and friends. The highest praise I can pay her is that the piece—even more moving now that one of the brothers has died—is deeply compassionate without being the least bit sentimental.

—Tom Marksbury

Scan the QR code to see the project online.

Career Discourse: Visual Podcast

Rachel Dixon

I think most of us in the WRD department know of Rachel and her work. I first met Rachel in my Multimedia Writing class and quickly realized that she would be that rare student who would be difficult for a teacher to challenge— but not because everything comes so easy for her, or that she finds easy ways around her problems. Rachel takes her challenges head on and finds creative and academically challenging ways to face them. Every assignment that she turned in to me surprised and delighted me with its layers of depth and significance. This particular assignment is the one I chose to nominate because it perfectly represents a larger ambition of Rachel's: to understand her own relationship to language and writing.

—Josh Abboud

Scan the QR code to see the project online.

Child Psychology in 10-to-11 Year Old Girl's Soccer

Isaac Michael Hayes

Isaac is a thoughtful and introspective student. He was an integral member of our WRD classroom, always offering pointed insight during discussions. His documentary made for my WRD 110 class, "Child Psychology in 10-to-11 Year Old Girl's Soccer," not only exhibited Isaac's academic prowess and rigorous work ethic, but it also showed his dedication to his soccer team on which the work was based. It was wonderful to see Isaac create such a caring and thoughtful documentary about the girls for whom he obviously has great affection. The documentary was a delightful example of theory intertwined with praxis, of the application of dense theoretical work to a very practical example. For this project, Isaac did the difficult work of combining scholarship with compassion. I am happy to have facilitated this work, but truly, it was all Isaac. His sensitive, academic contributions exhibit abilities that are rare for a person of his young age, and I was pleased to work with him to hone these skills.

—MaryAnn Kozlowski

Scan the QR code to see the project online.

Being Muslim in America: Who I Really Am

Shayna Holloway

When I asked my WRD 110 students to explore a local community for their final project, most of them chose a community to which they already belonged. In a class of 23, I received what seemed like endless advertisements for sororities, sports teams, and hometowns. However, some students decided to take a risk and explore communities they knew little about. Shayna went further. Not only did she choose a community of which she was not a member, but also she took the opportunity to educate the class about difference and inclusion, and to promote acceptance and kindness. In choosing to explore a community of young Muslim women in Kentucky, Shayna wanted to know what this community had to say about itself rather than speak on its behalf. She listened to members of this community and found that their experiences defy stereotypes. Each member was a unique individual whose identity should be respected. Shayna wanted to show the class that Islamaphobia is never acceptable, and education can lead to inclusion and understanding. While Shayna was researching her project, a mosque in Louisville was vandalized with hate-filled graffiti. Two months later, the Lexington Islamic Center received death threats. It seemed that hate and ignorance was on the rise in our community. However, in the midst of that hate, Shayna presented her project of hope and inclusion to the class. She showed them a video of several young Muslim women in Louisville happily chatting about their favorite things and then grimly discussing the bigotry they have faced. This was a message of hope but also a call for understanding and an end to baseless hatred.

—Lauren Copeland

Scan the QR code to see the project online.

Genre in True Detective: *The Agony and Delight of Expectation*

Richard Hooper

One of the things I treasure about teaching for WRD is the extremely fluid definition we apply to the word "writing." I have been given the great opportunity to construct classes on documentary production and what might be broadly called the rhetoric of popular culture. Richard's essay, which taught me a lot about one of my favorite media events ever—the first (emphasis on first) season of *True Detective*—is a fine illustration of this point. As an essay, it is a splendid piece of writing. But Richard, who wrote this for a class called "The New Television," keeps his argument focused mostly on non-verbal elements of the show, including composition, editing, and acting, and uses genre and reception theory in a highly sophisticated way to make us consider our own responses to what might initially seem to be a field ploughed well past exhaustion. His argument is refreshing, innovative, and speaks to what is so remarkable about so much of the new television beyond this one series.

—Tom Marksbury

True Detective has created a new high watermark in television for a number of distinct reasons, but one of the most important is the way it rewards viewers who are savvy about the genre it inhabits. The detective story is one of the most familiar in all of fiction, so it takes something truly unique to break the mold, and something even more distinctive to take that mold unto itself in a way that creates something truly new and exciting; *True Detective* succeeds at fitting both within and without the restrictions of genre, evoking some truly surprising aspects to the qualities it obtains. By utilizing character, setting, narrative structure, and even audience expectation, the story of Rustin Cohle and Martin Hart develops in thrilling ways that bend, break, and expand on its chosen genre.

Creator and writer Nic Pizzolatto both encourages and discourages immediate associations with the genre of the detective story and its subgenres, the murder mystery and the police procedural. By presenting a narrative framework that involves multiple stories, he draws us into the mystery of the murders that Rust and Hart are investigating in the past, but also into the personal drama that created the divide existing between them in the present. The investigation into the past case helps create associations we wouldn't have normally, demonstrating a wonderful technique of creating expectation and subverting it, as we hear the "official" version of events while witnessing the truth laid out underneath them. This device helps lead us to conclusions, truthful or not, but also encourages questions about the morality of the actions our protagonists take and the nature of their mental states both then and now.

Audience participation is something of an unspoken element of the detective story. Audiences have the desire to solve the mystery before it can be completely unraveled in the narrative, and *True Detective* employs one of the most dangerous red herrings as part of that process. The concept of one of the supposedly heroic protagonists secretly having been the murderer all along isn't new, but it's been done badly enough times that it's often a signal of poor quality in a work. Pizzolatto succeeds with it though, creating a dance around the possibility of Rust being the killer rather than the begrudging acknowledgement we've been trained to have as savvy viewers. This is the major entry point into the murder mystery genre for the show, as there are no clear suspects for us to consider in the early episodes, and Rust is presented as someone with more than a few strikingly odd habits. Even before the fallout between him and Marty, Rust is presented as someone who's unnerving: he constantly glares into a mirror just large enough to reflect a single eye, surrounds himself with nothing but materials about past murders, and even witnesses a haunting vision of one of the killer's symbols in the sky above a church that later yields a clue. While these can be seen as signs of Rust's entire being revolving around his ability as a detective, if they're removed from the knowledge of that role, they could just as easily be interpreted as signals of the kind of insanity we've been trained to associate with serial killer tropes. Even when taken in that context, they can suggest that. For example, he hangs around prostitutes, often favored victims in the genre, spurts meandering and strange philosophical monologues about the meaningless of life, and even quotes one of the criminals involved in the primary mystery with his repetition of Reggie Ledoux's assertion that "time is a flat circle." The latter occurs just minutes after we hear it from Ledoux himself, and as we see Rust conclude that the case goes past their current findings, we're subtly encouraged to believe that this shortcoming has broken him in some way.

By creating Rust as such an unusual character, embodying several of the typical patterns seen in perpetrators across the genre, the detectives interviewing him in the present directly echo at least some of our own suspicions as viewers as to his potential guilt. That safely insulates the story from the ineffectiveness of the last minute reveal, the norm for this genre, while also encouraging considerations about what exactly makes Rust and his partner "heroic." By allowing us to witness the objective reality of their experiences with the subjective reconstruction of them to the investigators, a dichotomy is born of Rust as a cop below the moral center of his profession, but above the capabilities of his peers within it. This is employed by both literal and figurative devices that help enhance our understanding of his character, ranging from his monologues to his resignation about taking a beating or having sex. In the lead up to one of the case's breakthroughs, Rust and Hart infiltrate a gang of bikers to gain information at the cost of participating in a theft from a drug den, and we see one of the most remarkable illustrations of Rust's character. Rust, a cop dressed as a criminal, uses Ginger, a criminal dressed like a cop, as a human shield when the heist goes sideways, simultaneously demonstrating his status as an outsider while twisting the expectations of the audience around.

The other side to this is Marty Hart's role, as a response to the anti-social inclinations of Rust, and the expectations an audience would have for a "typical" detective protagonist, and to the genre construction of the police procedural. Marty is more in the mode of the cliché private investigator, a hard drinking, hard living man who knows danger but is more than a little dangerous himself. The layer added on to that here is that Marty's life has continued past the point of the normal P.I. narrative in that he's become a family man; normally personal relationships with others outside the police are perfunctory parts of a police procedural, something granted to try and give characters an agency outside of their job. In that way, Marty's life from our perception begins when the stories of most detectives of his mode see theirs come to an end. His sleazy behavior and antiquated concepts of what being a man, husband, and authority entail help conceive a character several layers deeper than the legacy he's born from.

The specter of a savvy audience trying to outguess the mystery hangs over Hart's arc as well; his family life seems to be vaguely influenced by the time he's spending on the investigation in the past, and in the present their lives seem to have drastically improved in his absence. What family life fictional detectives are allowed is usually depicted simply, with relatively peaceful relationships sometimes enduring the trials of a particularly difficult case. Not so with Marty, as he comes into conflict with his wife for transgressions that exist far outside of his work, while still trying to use that as a justification for them. The case of Marty being a culprit is less strong than what's witnessed with Rust, but ultimately they've both committed crimes in the process of solving the mystery of the Yellow King, and that helps suggest a deeper moral endgame than normal genre vices like smoking or falling for the wrong woman. The latter is especially important, as the show demonstrates it with Marty's encounter with a young prostitute. His quick affair with her opens up the expectation that she'll be part of the mystery, the presence of a small devil statue in her room arguing for something sinister about her. Instead, Pizzolatto uses this burden of anticipation to further examine the raging cauldron of emotion present in Marty, another instance condemning the character's archaic and controlling mindset.

If Rust is the broken man who constantly evokes the things that damaged him in his speeches, Marty's responses are that of the man struggling to hold similar damage eternally within while resenting the weaknesses they represent. Marty is driven by emotions he's incapable of expressing, while Rust wants to express things in the hope it'll inspire the emotion he no longer feels. This can be related to the principles of the detective genre, as one half of the pair is resisting the development that has naturally been denied many of his predecessors, and the other is the greatest proponent of it. In doing this, Pizzolatto makes considerations for what the genre consists of, while attempting to transcend those limitations placed on it in its role there.

The locations in *True Detective* provide what's likely the strongest link to its genre forerunners; often in detective stories, the city has a character of its own, reflecting the story's themes or the characters' mindsets. This carries over to the empty fields and dingy structures of Louisiana seen here as well, though it's important to note that the long fields overflowing with swamp water represent less of Rust and Marty's mindset than they do the deep-rooted evil that they're pursuing. That's the major distinction from what audiences have come to know in other stories, as setting is often utilized to establish familiarity when it's employed here to evoke alienation, an ominous presence looming behind the actions of our heroes. By the end, the landscape has linked up with the field of stars that Rust and Marty look at after they recover from their encounter with Childress. Both serve as symbols of the great unknown evil that's beyond their ability to defeat completely and, while Rust refutes Marty's assertions that the darkness is winning, the dark sky above mirrors the corruption of the landscape they populate below. The stars, in turn, can be seen as representing the presence of people like Rust and Marty, or even successful cases solved among a greater unknown. The various interpretations available grant Pizzolatto's effort a far broader impact than the genre's familiar trope of the city as a sole extension of one character or theme.

Perhaps most daringly, in terms of its assigned genre, *True Detective* leans outside of its procedural roots into the realm of personal philosophy. Rust Cohle might come across as a purely nihilistic individual who's resigned to fatalistic decay, but that firm mantra is eroded by his experiences in Childress' labyrinth; instead of finding his pessimistic views reinforced by how the murders are connected to something much larger and likely unstoppable, Rust sees his life reaffirmed, coming out the other side more hopeful than he had been since his daughter died. Often a detective's back story is a minor part of a show's premise, a device to differentiate him in some unique way, or even to echo familiarity with other characters in that same mode. *True Detective* provides that as well but takes it one step further: that background is what ultimately allows Rust to change. By limiting the show's narrative to this one story, Pizzolatto gives both Rust and Marty the chance to transcend the status quo limitations of genre; they evolve beyond the roles of the skeptic and the cynic. The rage and tension that defined their relationship fades away to form complete arcs for them as individuals, as well as preserving their place as classical "hard men" in a time that has left their attitudes behind.

What's most shocking about all of this is that, ultimately, it can be argued that the mystery supposedly at the core of the story is perfunctory and functions more as the window dressing for the psychological breakdown and philosophical contest between these men and the world they inhabit. The murders are an engine that moves the plot forward, and an important element that helps the two men reunite and change, but the ambiguity, given the effectiveness of the resolution, is an active rejection of the tidiness of most mystery stories. In turn, many dismissed the show's conclusion as defeatist and cowardly; running away from the larger ambitions the narrative implied, it ultimately misses the element which allowed it to break free of the restrictions of genre: the characters. One of the most noteworthy elements of both Rust and Marty's arcs is that they're ultimately morally deficient people. Rust is alienating to most people, barely able to hold himself together at times, and Marty is such a negative force in the lives of his family that they seem far happier once he's been removed from them. That level of difficulty of character isn't one frequently applied to the detective genre, as its characters are often ciphers for the gradual unfolding of a mystery rather than fully formed individuals with moral agency and ambiguity about them. Efforts have been made in the past, but they have always been secondary to the driving force behind the genre, the mysteries that move things forward. The narrative device of the stories in the past, present, and time in between helps generate an ongoing mystery with twists unto itself, while providing a greater opportunity to create exciting layers not seen in the genre before. The toxic masculinity of Marty is just as valuable as the defeatist pessimism of Rust, and both are explored thoroughly in ways that other stories of this ilk would never approach, as they serve as affectations rather than arenas of genuine interest.

All of these factors contribute to the show transcending both the boundaries of the detective genre and its respective subgenres, as well as the burden of audience expectation that's generated by those classifications. *True Detective* leans into a striking new arena of genre hybrid: the psychological detective drama. By structuring the narrative around the past and present, truth and reality, new touchstones of potential are uncovered both for a type of story long acclimated to no longer challenging itself, as well as for the viewers who have witnessed that gradual stagnation. Playing with what we know and don't know simultaneously, the show both typifies and denies the familiar elements of genre and surpasses them in its depictions of riveting characters in a singularly intimidating landscape that is unfolded by a storytelling device that plays up these strengths heavily. *True Detective* isn't "just" a detective story, as it completely avoids the downfall of its contemporaries where thrill and emotion ultimately evaporate once the mystery is solved or ultimate fates are revealed. Instead, it navigates new depths and daringly frustrates those who approach it is as they would those other works.

Rhetorical Analysis

Zach Jolly

In my WRD 111 class the students analyzed advertisements, understanding how ads work as arguments using various rhetorical techniques. In this rhetorical analysis, Zach looks at three Fiat ads. In analyzing them, Zach manages to see not only the discrete parts of ads and the techniques associated with each part, but also how those parts work both with and against each other to create a unified whole and advance a specific message. Zach not only looks at how the parts work in the ads, but is able to explain how they work within their specific contexts while targeting various audiences, identifying and explaining the various techniques used for these shifting goals. He also explains how the advertisers shape audience perception and how they use certain features to guide the eye, forcing viewers to read it as they intend. Zach covers a lot of ground in rather limited space, his analysis both deep and concise.

—JJ Roberts

The Fiat car company has been in business since post World War II and has clung to its Italian heritage ever since its beginning. Fiat has only recently marketed toward an American audience. As a result, it has had to come up with a new marketing strategy. Since 2011 Fiat has used an edgy, young, and adventurous approach on its American market ("Introducing"). Fiat marketing has taken on a reputation as being some of the most enjoyed ads by all Americans. This includes years of Fiat entertaining millions during their highly anticipated Super Bowl commercials. Through these analyses, I will break down the Fiat ads in a unique way. Rather than going into fine detail about what their commercials say, I will evaluate how Fiat has become such a popular company in America's cut-throat advertising competitions. The main elements of a Fiat ad include different emphases on the rhetorical triangle. This emphasis includes logos, an appeal to logic which includes statistics and facts; pathos, an emotional appeal which fiat typically uses as desire and humor; and ethos, an appeal to Fiat's credibility. There are a few other strategies used that will be looked at, but these are the main focus of Fiat's ads.

(Reising)

The ad featured on the left is very typical of how Fiat advertises to a particular audience. In this case, the audience is heterosexual males, approximately in their twenties or thirties. However, I believe the case could be made equally for a younger teenage male audience, despite the fact that they are not necessarily in the market for car buying. This ad was placed in an ESPN magazine and thus confirms the assertion that the audience is really only younger males. However, even without that context, the desired audience can still be deduced. The first and most obvious piece of evidence is the female referee placed in the foreground. It is important to note that she is dressed seductively with short shorts and bent over in order to show cleavage. The girl is in the foreground because she is the main reason the audience will take a second look at the ad. She also represents both pathos and ethos appeals. The first rhetorical element is the sexuality placed in the ad. It actually can be linked to the next "step" in the ad. The referee is looking directly at the man driving the car, and the viewer is supposed to follow her eyes to the car.

Moreover, the car itself is an analogy for a football player. The reason for the faulty analogy is to show a parallelism in the smaller size of the Fiat Abarth, and a smaller football running back, both of which are supposed to represent power and toughness (Cross). This again relates back to the pathos appeal riddled throughout the ad. The viewers see themselves in the car, which will then give them the feeling of being powerful and the ability to attract women like the one on the ad.

As for ethos, the model in the ad is a representation of all attractive women when viewed from the perspective of a young male. This model is essentially endorsing a car by showing that men can win women's attention by driving a Fiat. This, of course, is a faulty endorsement, but in the eyes of the beholder, who is compromised by the pathos appeals, she is in fact a representation of all women.

The third rhetorical triangle piece (logos) is the least important to this specific ad. This is evident because all the facts that are used to sell the car are placed in the bottom right corner in white font, which is overshadowed by the red font that promises unlimited female attraction. The statistic given is about the torque the Fiat can produce. Fiat was a lot more concerned about giving a picture of how power looks than actually telling the audience facts about the car itself. Only a reader who closely studied all aspects of the ad would have noticed this statistic. Clearly this ad focuses more on pathos and ethos than giving consumers a logical reason to buy a product.

> "(1) It gave Italians the ability to move freely as they recovered from WWII …. (2) It encourages people to be in charge of their lives, live assertively and celebrate the smallest of things with infectious excitement …. (3) The Fiat 500 has earned more than 80 international awards, including the 2008 European car of the year … ("Introducing").

However, Fiat does not completely ignore the viewers who are more susceptible to a logical appeal. Their website provides a greater connection between pathos and logos. One section of the website is labeled as history. In this section, Fiat has a chance to define who they are and to establish their own credibility. The first quote is one of the first sentences in a short article about Fiat's history; it is also the first of nine times that Italy is mentioned. What Fiat wants is for its audience to see that Italy is essential to their identity. Fiat does this to make their car seem better. A Fiat is not the typical car found in America; they are much smaller than their competitors. Fiat knows that they cannot compete as an American car, so they must show that they are special by building their identity around Italy. Once the consumer hears this repeatedly, Fiat becomes synonymous with Italy. Thus the car is no longer abnormal, but instead it is foreign or exotic. Fiat uses Italy as a euphemism for small.

In this quote there is also the mention of WWII. Yes, this is a vital part of their history, but they are careful to mention WWII on their American specific website. This is in fact an attempt to show some connection between America and Italy. This is a common argumentative technique called appealing to tradition. Fiat wants their American audience to know that Italy and America share a common bond from the war. World War II is also something Americans take pride in. This feeling of pride is an attempt for Fiat to use pathos as a way to win over their audience. The idea of drawing similarities between the two cultures is something Fiat does quite often. In the previous advertisement we saw Fiat comparing their small Italian car to a small American running back. Both of these examples show an attempt for Fiat to say that their Italian product is actually quite similar to American values. This may seem contradictory to the original assertion that Fiat is trying to flaunt its foreign appeal, but in actuality, the two are working in tandem. The foreign appeal is only surface deep. In order to attract the most customers, just enough Italian appeal is put in for the owner to say, "Oh, look at my fancy foreign car," but yet the ad contains enough Americanization for that customer to not worry about appearing too different. Fiat is also appealing to that same customer's sense of adventure, which stirred up his or her initial interest in buying something a little different.

The second quote gets to the very core of Fiat's identity, which is to have fun and live adventurously. Again, this is full of pathos and is intended to stir up emotions of desire to live like a Fiat owner would. The audience would then see buying a Fiat as the next logical step to gain that lifestyle. Also, we again see that Fiat recognizes that it is a challenge to sell such a different car in an American environment. As a result, they attack the challenge head on by saying that people who live assertively and are in charge also take pride in small things … like a Fiat. Therefore, the audience now feels better about buying this car that is actually being endorsed by the ideal take-charge person that they have conjured up in their mind. Of course that source is going to be credible to each and every person. After all, they are the ones who created that ideal person.

In between all of this ethos and pathos, Fiat also brings in some logical appeal. Fiat ends their introduction with a fact that, in summary, says Fiat is a popular car and they have awards to prove it. This is an example of Fiat utilizing logic and ethos together. For a reader to become a customer, they must be convinced that the car is in fact a quality car. Fiat places their awards in front of the reader and convinces them that they are a credible company. Thus, the logic that created the ethos is then used again as logos by making the case that it makes sense to buy from this world-renowned car company. The same technique is used in the previous example as well. Fiat used a model to represent all women, then showed their audience a car owner getting unlimited attention from "all women." It then became easy for the reader to come to the faulty, but seemingly logical, conclusion that buying the car will warrant attention from all women. Both cases have Fiat leading you right to the edge of an illogical conclusion. All the audience has to do is fall down a seemingly logical path.

In order to see the best ads that this company uses, it would make sense to look at the biggest stage for advertisements. Since Fiat started marketing in America, they have taken advantage of the Super Bowl commercial war. Last year's ad was one of the most popular and features a middle-aged man being enticed by his lover. He goes into the bathroom to take what is perceived to be a male enhancement pill. He tries to throw it into his mouth, but instead the pill flies out the window and bounces around Italian architecture until it finds its way into a Fiat's gas cap. The Fiat then grows into the newer and bigger model for 2015 ("Official").

(Dinawitay)

The goal of the commercial war is to have the most talked about advertisement of the night. What follows is a vast array of attention from talk show hosts and celebrities. Some advertisers try to use the ethos appeal to win over the audience, but most have found that the best way to win is to evoke a pathos appeal of either sadness or humor. Being the fun and adventurous company that they are, Fiat chose humor. According to Michigan State University advertising professors, the careful planning and $4.5 million paid off by not just winning Fiat a victory in the ad wars but also additional endorsements and publicity like the attention they gained from being chosen as the best Super Bowl ad by MSU faculty (VanHulle). In order to defend their reputation for having a great Super Bowl ad, Fiat used their qualities that are seen in each advertisement above, only this time it is adapted for humor. Recall the model in the first ad and how she was placed in a way to sexualize and attract men towards her and then ultimately the car. Sex is still a common base for this commercial, except this time instead of using a young model to seduce young men, two middle aged Italian adults are used. The goal here was to attract the audience to the car with laughter, not seduction. Fiat has a reputation for using sexuality, in their Super Bowl ads, that would change to be more along the lines of the first ad by using the middle aged models; there is an irony involved that the viewer finds funny. Fiat also notes that the audience is much larger and diverse than an ESPN magazine. With a larger audience comes a much greater risk of using a sexualized model. There is a fear of backlash from feminist and other groups who would be against the subjection of women as objects. So, they completely took away the seduction and blatant sex appeal for an ad that just hints around the idea. This is also safer for younger audience members who will not know what a "blue pill" is for. By not offending this larger audience, they can trust that the audience will talk about their hilarious ad the next day to all their friends.

Fiat also is very careful to keep their identity locked into each of their ads. The man and woman both have tanner complexions and give off the idea that they are Italian themselves. The scene where the pill is bouncing around outside on rooftops also shows Italy. The buildings are older looking and made of stone. Even the man's house is a yellow stone color with shutters. This is giving the impression that the pill is bouncing around Italy. Although Fiat does not explicitly say Italy over and over again like they do on their website, they do hint at it constantly. Again this is to make the audience feel that this car has a foreign appeal to it. In fact, Fiat is so recognizable as being Italian that the audience of the first ad would be comfortable making the assertion that the female referee is actually Italian herself. Nothing directly says that she is, but then again her dark hair and skin complexion will not argue against the assumptions.

Fiat also incorporates their free lifestyle into the ad, but of course in a more comical way. In the first ad we saw Fiat appealing to young men with a football scene that would produce feelings of adventure and toughness, while on Fiat's website they directly expressed that their car was made for adventurous and free individuals who take charge. Those ideas come across as humorous in this ad because of the two middle-aged individuals trying to live those values out. The man has on a flamboyant cheetah print robe and the woman has on a red lacey gown. The woman is trying to be spontaneous and exciting by surprising the man, which are all the ideas that Fiat uses to attract younger audiences. However, the ad constantly reminds us that despite these two trying to live a young and free life, they are still restricted by their age. This is where the man's grey hair and beard play in, and the fact that he needs to even take his blue pill. This is where the comedy comes into the picture. By making the audience laugh and feel good, they are making it harder for the viewer to say no to the product and even harder to at least advertise this commercial to their friends. It is important to notice that the use of a middle-aged couple in a mid-life crisis is not directly related to Fiat in any way. This is to make sure that the intended young adult audience is still confident that the car is designed for them and not their parents. In actuality, this ad makes fun of that middle-aged couple and the fact that their moment went terribly wrong. This of course further separates Fiat from older audiences and further secures them with the younger demographic.

Fiat has become a master of advertisements ever since the car was reintroduced in America. They have been able to make a name for themselves based on the ideas of freedom and adventure, while heavily using pathos to do so. Although each ad fluctuates in its use of appeals to ethos and logos, they all rely on an emotional appeal to target their audience. Even the pathos varied between ads as a way to make sure the target audience was being catered to. In each case, Fiat was careful to give them what they wanted: the first being attraction, the second was appealing to desires of adventure, and the third being devoted completely to humor. They have been able to adapt their car to America through advertising, and have produced ads that most people actually look forward to seeing.

Works Cited

Cross, Donna. "Propaganda: How Not To Be Bamboozled." Web. 10 Mar. 2015.

Dinawitay. "(Video) Sexy Fiat 2015 Superbowl Commercial." *Stunnalife*. 1 Feb. 2015. Web. 16 Mar.

"Introducing the All-New FIAT® 500X." *FIAT Nation*. Web. 5 Feb. 2015.

"Official 2015 FIAT 500X Super Bowl Commercial "The FIAT Blue Pill #500X." *YouTube*. Web. 5 Feb. 2015.

Reising, Matt. "FIAT Abarth in ESPN Magazine." *On The Digital Age*. Web. 2 Mar. 2015.

VanHulle, Lindsay. "MSU Profs Rank Fiat's 'Blue Pill' Ad Best of Super Bowl." *Lansing State Journal*. Web. 10 Mar. 2015.

On the Spectrum

Manuel (Tre) Roy Lyerly III

I asked the class to explore issues of community, difference, and identity for their individual documentary projects in WRD 110. Tre's approach to this assignment demonstrates what an incredibly creative, intelligent, and thoughtful student he is. Tre expertly edited his work, and he even recorded his own background music. Tre was also the only student I've ever taught who actually managed to get audible gasps of surprise out of the class during his documentary presentation. Tre opened his presentation by interacting with a recording he'd made of himself and the two Tres introduced in his short documentary, "On the Spectrum." The film asks the simple question, "What is autism and why are people with it different?" What follows is a fascinating and approachable exploration of his experiences with an autism spectrum disorder. Tre personalizes spectrum disorders by showing how autism is as varied and unique as the individuals who have it. Tre also relates his experience dealing with stereotypes to broader examples of how other UK students face a wide range of stereotypes. Tre's work weaves his research together with humor, personal stories, and engaging interviews to present a complex and endearing view of his experiences as someone with an autism spectrum disorder.

—Danielle Dodson

Scan the QR code to see the project online.

Disability on Campus

David Mynheer

Students in this WRD 110 class were asked to create a blog that explored, through narratives and visuals, a person or community in their life that was representative of difference. David was eager from the beginning to take on this task by chronicling a community he is a member of, University of Kentucky college students with disabilities. In his blog, David tactfully exposes the challenges members of this community face everyday through photographs taken from his point of view, accompanied by compelling narratives that point out just how far this campus has to go before it is truly accessible. David's work shows that he is passionate about using rhetoric to make a difference in his community. Through David's resilience and talent for writing, I have no doubt that he will continue to be a force for positive change as he works toward his ultimate goal of becoming an English teacher.

—Eleanor Feltner

Scan the QR code to see the project online.

Seven Tenths: A Family Portrait

Maria Reist

Maria Reist's wry and moving "Seven Tenths: A Family Portrait" captures the joys and underlying tensions of life in a large family with a skilled eye for the anecdote and an amazing emotional clarity—especially since hers is the large family in question. Using rapid-fire editing to let the individual brothers and sisters speak for themselves while still telling their story as a group, Maria takes the old verity "show, don't tell" to heart. The aggregate of their various narratives is testimony to both the richness and the complications of growing up with so many siblings.

—Tom Marksbury

Scan the QR code to see the project online.

Rhetorical Analysis of Mathews Garden

Daniela H. Rivera

In a world of constant digital and media stimuli, what value does the natural world hold? Daniela Rivera's "A Rhetorical Analysis of Mathews Garden" explores an easily overlooked and contentious space on the University of Kentucky's campus. Rivera pays particular attention to the ways in which familiar, everyday spaces can be re-viewed and re-seen after conducting close observation and outside research. She argues that natural spaces, like Mathews Garden, can and should be considered local memorials and living monuments to our state's and university's past and future. Rivera synthesizes the perspectives of local historians, professors, and students in addition to weaving in her own detailed observations gleaned from time spent in the garden. This project raises questions about the politics embedded in local and campus spaces. For example, what continues the border between forest and city, urban and rural? What is the future of our campus and local green spaces? Who gets to decide how land is used and for what purposes? What impact do green spaces make on humans and vice versa?

—Mary Clai Jones

Hidden between the University of Kentucky's Law Building and Mineral and Mining building lies a quiet haven known to a few as the Mathews Garden. Within the confines of a white, wooden, slightly eroded fence lies a naturalist's dream. In the spring and summer, the buds of the plants burst through the dredges of snow left from the past winter, and the Mathews

Garden is transformed into a lush, beautiful landscape of a variety of plants from different regions of the country and parts of the world living in close proximity. Plants from the American Holly to bamboo can be found within the confines of the Mathews Garden. And yet even for all of its beauty, the Mathews Garden is not very well-known to the community. Tucked away between two buildings, the Mathews Garden can easily be overlooked. As a result, this haven of colors and luscious smells is in danger of being torn down. The Mathews Garden exists as a historical marker of the university and brings into question the preservation versus expansion of a location. Should tradition be sacrificed for the monumental movement of the modern? Or should we work to preserve the memory of what once was, in order to educate those who come after?

The Mathews House and Garden are relics of a period in the university's history, and yet they were set for demolition in 2012 in order to expand the College of Law. In an article from the Kentucky Kernel, Bob Wiseman, the vice president of UK Facilities stated, "the university must utilize our limited available space very carefully and strategically" (Kayla Pickrell, 2012). The demolition was postponed, however, with the help of The Blue Grass Trust for Historic Preservation. It's a trust whose goal is to preserve historical houses like the Mathews House. It started in 1955 when the group of individuals first saved the Hunt-Morgan house from demolition and restored it to its original 1814 appearance (About the Blue Grass Trust, 2015).

The Mathews House is one of the many historical houses that can be found in Lexington. The house and the garden once belonged to a Clarence Wentworth Mathews who was the first Dean of the College of Agriculture in the early 1900s. The Mathews House and Garden honor his memory and the legacy he gave to the university. During his time as the Dean of the College of Agriculture, he and his daughter Ruth began the garden. In 1968 when Mathews passed away, Ruth gave the garden to the University of Kentucky. The job of tending the garden was passed to a biology professor, James Krupp, who continues to take care of it today (Save Golden Glory, 2015).

Perhaps the location of the Mathews Garden is not the optimal spot. Between two buildings, it is easy to overlook it. I was never aware of its existence either. A trip to the Mathews Garden is what made me fall in love with it. The sights and smells of the garden were so convoluted, and yet its what made it come alive to me. I have read that some consider the garden "wild" (Save Golden Glory, 2015), and yet nowhere else can you find a garden that has so many species of plant life from around the world in one place. The Mathews Garden is distinctly one of a kind. As a result, there are arguments that can be made to preserve this garden. In Erik Reece's Lexington Herald-Leader article he explains the magnitude of diversity and variety that can be found in this garden. Reece urges that the fact that the garden contains "350 different species of flora is one of the strongest reasons for its preservation." He adds that, "the garden is a teaching laboratory for classes from the sciences like dendrology and ecology" (Save Golden Glory, 2015). Other articles agree with Reece's article, like Morgan Eads' article in the Kentucky Kernel which states, "The garden also attracts many species of migratory birds" (Professor Speaks Out Against Garden Removal, 2015). The garden is a valuable source of education with the diversity and variety it provides within its walls. Likewise, because of the background that the garden shares with the house, it can also provide an education in other areas that do not pertain to science.

Considering the history of the Mathews House and the garden, the garden and the house can also attract those studying the history of the community around them. The Mathew House stands by its garden and represents physically a period of the university that has surpassed a bit of time. Studying the garden and the house would pose great interest to those whose interests lie in the history of the school. Reece's article agrees that, "the Mathews Garden is a remainder of what we once were, as Kentuckians and human beings" (Save Golden Glory, 2015). Organizations such as the Blue Grass Trust exist because of the individuals who advocate for the preservation of these places. Those on campus who can see the value of the garden and house should advocate for it and for other places like the Mathews House.

With the campus continuing to build and expand, many of the pockets of nature amongst the cement walls are dwindling. There is beauty that can be seen in the mix between what is natural and what is manmade.

The Mathews Garden brings into question a very important idea of what should be preserved and what should be expanded on. However, it can also be interpreted as a debate between the traditional versus the modern. Lexington is a developing, young city that still contains many of its roots and heritage. The Mathews House represents the memory of some of that heritage. Therefore, the demolition of the Mathews House and garden would be a loss to Lexington's cultural heritage. What will Lexington sacrifice in order to gain this modern image? The question is not just centralized in Lexington, but in communities around the country and the world. In New York City the MOMA (Modern Museum of Art) recently demolished a Folk Art Building in order to make room for a connection to the Tower Verre that houses three floors of another collection. The demolition of the Folk Art Building caused a roaring consensus among art politics disagreeing with its actions. Michael Sorkin wrote in a news source, *The Nation,* how this act was "a disrespect to revered traditions" (MOMA Adrift, 2014). The controversial topic of preserving tradition versus advancement in the modern is a continuous debate. The debate will probably never end, but as individuals with voices, we must continue to voice our opinions about subjects in order to have a say in their outcomes.

In reference to the Mathews Garden, it represents an important historical landmark to the university and the students who attend it. Perhaps its location is not optimal, but the university can do more to publicize its location and the location of other landmarks on campus. It is of great value to the school, from the lush wildlife study that it provides the students in the sciences, to the history lesson it can provide the rest of the student body on its own university. As individuals it is important to remember that as the community continues to expand, that the individuals in the community should protect the things that came before.

Works Cited

Eads, Morgan. "Professor Speaks Out Against Garden Removal." *KyKernal.* Kentucky Kernal, 12 Oct. 2012. Web. 12 Mar. 2015.

Lewis, Michael. "MOMA Adrift." *EBSCOHOST.* EBSCOHOST, 1 May 2014. Web. 12 Mar. 2015.

Pickrell, Kayla. "UK Could Demolish 2 Historical Campus Sites." *Kentucky Kernel.* 28 Aug. 2012. Web. 20 Mar. 2015.

Reece, Erik. "Save Golden Glory of 660: Biophilia Thrives in Wild of UK's Mathews Garden." *Lexington Herald Leader.* 4 May 2014. Web. 12 Mar. 2015.

"What We Do." *About The Blue Grass Trust.* Web. 12 Mar. 2015.

The Power in the Unspoken

Robin Spratling

When I designed a WRD 111 course around memorials and public memory last year, I was a little nervous about the potential challenges of trying to get students to think critically about memorials. Robin's essay, "The Power in the Unspoken," immediately proved my fears wrong. Robin argued that there was a problematic absence of controversy surrounding the Confederate monument at Stone Mountain, Georgia, and she connected this absence to a larger problem with memory in the South. Robin's essay was well researched and beautifully written, but what stood out to me most was how she transformed this analytical essay into a call for action. Robin insisted that continued silence on this Confederate monument was as good as support for the racist cause these men represented, and she concluded that our indifference to the symbolism behind Stone Mountain was parallel to the lack of accountability for racism in America today. Robin continued to grapple with the complex issues surrounding memory and race for her group documentary project, in which she and her group members explored public memory around victims of police brutality. Robin is a deeply engaged, creative, and thoughtful student and writer, and I am so proud of her work in WRD 111.

—Danielle Dodson

Situated just sixteen miles from the metropolitan area of Atlanta, a city that many consider the face of the New South, sits one of the world's largest monuments, a rock carving on the face of Stone Mountain. The subject of this famous rock carving: three Confederate soldiers. In an area that is predominantly black, the idea of a Confederate soldier memorial, celebrating the efforts of those soldiers who fought to keep slavery in the South, seems wrong, almost like placing a monument recognizing the Nazis as heroes in the middle of Jewish Israel. Despite how seemingly backwards this monument is, there is little controversy surrounding it. It is as if it is just another facet of the landscape, left unquestioned by most. The Stone Mountain region, like the rest of the south, has a long history of racism which is perpetuated through the carving on the face of the mountain. A lack of opposition to the monument is much like the South's neglect of problems of prejudice and oppression that still exist in the region.

In his "I Have a Dream" speech, Martin Luther King Jr. stated, "let freedom ring from Stone Mountain of Georgia" (King). The inclusion of Stone Mountain in his speech was intentional due to its long history of racism as one of the Ku Klux Klan's primary meeting places. The KKK is known for cross burning and lynchings atop Stone Mountain, and they continued their annual rallies until the early nineties (Morse, et al.). The Klan represents the worst of racism in the South; however, other aspects of Stone Mountain's history are not to be discarded. The carving itself, which depicts three highly ranked Confederates—Jefferson Davis, Robert E. Lee, and Thomas "Stonewall" Jackson—was originally drafted and funded by the United Daughters of the Confederacy (Hale 23). All aspects of the monument represent oppression, past and present, in the Southern United States, and although the Civil Rights movement ended in the 60s, anti-black sentiments and outward expressions like this, ranging from discreet to blatant, are pervasive within our culture.

Although the monument incorporates various racist elements, it is supported by many. Petitions to destroy the carving, like those made by an African American Atlantan named McCartney Forde in 2013, were not widely supported. For Forde, the Confederate memorial is "like a black eye" within Stone Mountain Park and in Atlanta (Jauregi). He expressed that "there should be a memorial that we can all be proud of" (11 Alive News). Many Georgians do not see it this way. In fact, many see petitions like Forde's as an effort to erase history. "Revisionist history," as regarded negatively by many, effectively sugar-coats our past and causes us to forget what made us who we are today.

This issue surrounding the monument, however, goes beyond the question of "revising history." The problem is that it celebrates these men as national heroes. These soldiers were the same men who fought for slavery during the Civil War, and they supported violence towards black Americans. In a post-Civil Rights America, these men should not be held up as heroes. In spite of their bravery as soldiers, what they stood for was morally reprehensible in today's culture. As we memorialize these men, we are supporting their cause. Although there are people who support the monument on Stone Mountain, the vast majority of Atlantans are indifferent to it. This group of people is the most important demographic because their silence results in a society that continues to oppress those who have been "free" since Abraham Lincoln issued the Emancipation Proclamation in 1863.

Inaction condones wrongdoings. A trend of silence, as well as failure to acknowledge that racism is deeply embedded within our culture, is occurring across our Nation, and it goes far beyond the issue of whether or not the Confederate monument should remain on the face of Stone Mountain. A problem of national indifference allows racism to continue into the twenty-first century, despite the fact that the Civil Rights Movement ended almost fifty years ago. Nothing will ever change if white Americans continue to neglect the problems of racism within the United States.

As a white American, it is easy to forget that the color of our skin shapes our daily interactions and lifestyles, affects our ability to not blink an eye at the sight of a Confederate flag waving on a neighbor's front porch, and gives us the privilege to remain silent against the oppression that also shapes the lives of our black counterparts. Recent events in Ferguson, Missouri with the police shooting of Michael Brown or the Trayvon Martin case bring a conversation that has been a part of the black community for decades to the forefront of American media. The problem of underlying racism has been occurring in our country for many years, but has been largely pushed aside and disregarded by whites.

Going beyond even the idea of police brutality, racial injustices continue to be institutionalized within places of work, our education system, our prisons, and every other aspect of our public lives. These inequalities have become impossible to ignore with blacks and hispanics comprising 58% of the incarcerated population, while they only make up 25% of the general population (NAACP.org). Whites still earn on average over $10,000 more annually than blacks. This disparity only increased after the economic recession in 2011, and schools still remain effectively segregated across our nation. What is more concerning, however, is that schools with populations that are primarily white are better funded than those containing more black students (Plumer). "All men are created equal" is stated in our Declaration of Independence; however, if you take a closer look at our nation, it is anything but equal. In spite of these clear inequalities, white Americans continue to ignore the differences between the races and often times even put the blame on black Americans, claiming that it is "a cultural problem," and that the black population should be able to "pull themselves up from their bootstraps." However, the cultural problem is not among African Americans, but among whites. Even those who do not actively participate in putting down the oppressed have a responsibility to take action and say something about the maltreatment that takes place every day in every community across the Nation.

The issue that arises when discussing the Confederate Memorial on the face of Stone Mountain is much more complex than simply honoring those who fought to maintain the right to own slaves in the 1860s. A lack of controversy surrounding the seemingly questionable monument is a controversy in itself. The refusal to acknowledge the monument as another form of oppression within our society is much like what white Americans do everyday without oftentimes realizing it, perpetuating centuries-long oppression. It is with silence and inaction that police brutality against blacks, educational inequalities, and overarching racist sentiments continue to pervade every aspect of our society. Much like the carving on the face of Stone Mountain, prejudices and discrimination are etched, carved, and go without notice in the United States every day.

Works Cited

"Criminal Justice Fact Sheet." *NAACP.org.* n.d. Web. 25 February 2015.

Hale, Elizabeth Grace. "Granite Stopped Time: The Stone Mountain Memorial and the Representation of White Southern Identity." *The Georgia Historical Quarterly* Vol. 82, No. 1 (SPRING 1998). Georgia Historical Society. pp. 22–44. Web. JSTOR. 20 February 2015.

Jauregi, Andres. "Stone Mountain Petition Stokes Controversy; Georgia Man Wants Confederate Monument Remade." *The Huffington Post.* 25 February 2015. Web.

King, Martin L. "American Rhetoric: Martin Luther King, Jr.—I Have a Dream." *American Rhetoric: The Power of Oratory in the United States.* Intellectual Properties Management, n.d. Web. 20 February 2015.

Morse, Minna and Maggie Steber. "The changing face of Stone Mountain." *Smithsonian* Vol. 29 Issue 10. Web. Academic Search Complete. 22 February 2015.

Plumer, Brad. "These ten charts show the black-white economic gap hasn't budged in 50 years." *The Washington Post.* 28 August 2013. Web. 25 February 2015.

11 Alive News. "Petition wants Stone Mt. carving removed." Online video clip. *Youtube.* 1 May 2013. Web. 20 February 2015.

Behind Cubicle Walls: The Tale of an Audio File and Its Place in the Work Force

Kristi Mary Ronna Street

I first met Kristi Street in Work Stories, a class I teach about labor and rhetoric. She is an excellent student, a talented writer, and, most importantly, an original thinker. I always look forward to reading her assignments because I know they will be interesting. In a response to the final assignment for this class, which asked students to tell a story about work in the medium of their choice, Kristi created a unique sound essay. In this piece, sounds of the office and the construction outside reveal the narrator's surprisingly ambivalent feelings about her job.

—Katherine Rogers-Carpenter

Scan the QR code to see the project online.

Synthpop and Hip

Joseph Torres

This piece comes from a course I have been privileged to create for WRD, "The History of Hip," which takes as its reason for being the notion that Hip is not some ephemeral passing fashion or fancy but a lasting rich and deep alternative culture. I try to give students as broad a range of subjects as I can, and Joseph Torres, who was also a standout student in my course on Television, ingeniously dug into something most people might casually dismiss, or be unable to articulate in any critical way. Music can be daunting to analyze, and synthpop maybe more than most, but Joseph is able to deploy traditionally literary critical methods, synthesize them with the philosophical concerns John LeLand raises in our text, *Hip: the History,* and virtually re-invent the way we think about how this subgenre intersects with identity. I would also like to mention Joseph's nearly-as-good other essay for this class, which advanced what seemed to me the rather unpromising argument that T. S. Eliot's "The Wasteland" is hip. He was right, I was wrong. Joseph, you ought to be a lawyer if you can win that one.

—Tom Marksbury

As a genre, synthpop has a deep origin in the early eighties instrumentation--the use of sequencers—while ignoring things like MIDI soundtracks. In their original form, they focused on a sense of ironic "detachment" songs that shared the notion of losing someone or something you cared about, but this was done as a reversal or rejection of that same media. If you sang about a girlfriend leaving you, then you were mocking the culture in which one would be sad if abandoned by a female associate. In the late 2000s, this genre of music experienced something beyond a renaissance, entering something that many would call its heyday. It became deeply intertwined with the emotions of nostalgia and longing for the eighties, in both an ironic and sincere way. It shared a visual aesthetic with retrofuturism, as well as cyberpunk, evoking a deep, dark future. The largest departure from the original synthpop/synthwave tone is that now those same emotions that were being mocked have become legitimate and genuine. It has reached a strange hybrid, where loving the aesthetic is both sincere and sarcastic; in a lot of ways this is reflected in how people view films from the eighties as well. (We've all heard someone say, "It's so bad, it's good.") In this way, synthpop is very hip; it has a strong underground culture, made up of people who make the music themselves, often at home or alone, with a certain emphasis on an aesthetic over function. Even the sarcastic embrace of genuine is so fluid and hybrid, that something about it seems impossible but also effortless.

Synthpop/synthwave (used interchangeably for the course of this work) falls into a set of tropes and ideas about how music should sound, how it should look, and how it should be made. It has a sense of "unclean production"; the sound quality often isn't perfect or concise, but instead, is deliberately left unaltered. The structure is usually minimal, holding to a specific series of sounds and beats repeatedly. The equipment requires one to use analog synthesizers and drum machines that were produced in the seventies and eighties to get the appropriate sound. The beat is typically mechanical and machine-like; it's easy to pick up and follow. The patterns are usually quite repetitive and broken up into very short sections rather than long complex parts. The drum beats themselves are programmed to sound more digital and synthesized, while thin, trebled melodies are used to portray the artificial series of sounds that are being produced, rather than avoid it. The vocal portions are set up in such a way to counter this, to add a distinctly human or organic feeling. Primarily, synthpop focused on an an aesthetic influenced by constructivism, which focused on art as a social product, rather than a purely musical endeavor. The literature of existentialism usually found itself among friends in synthwave, and science fiction is very important as well. Lastly, the music founded the sort of image of doing it yourself; most of the artists produced in small home studios, in even smaller batches of cassettes or vinyl, covered with art that they had made themselves, or had associates produce.

In the following attempt to dissect synthpop as a hip construct, this essay will be divided into segments. The first will discuss the artist Kavinsky, whose work shares the closest lineage with the original structure. Next, is the exploration of sub-genres, though primarily these will come in three classes: darkwave, with Perturbator as its high priest; chillwave, where Toro y Moi had all the influence; and lastly, vaporwave, as it flowed from Blank Banshee. In each case, the artists will be discussed according to how they contribute to a particular scene or "aesthetic," and how they are hip; the points of discussion will primarily include who they are as an artist, how their music is produced, how it is sold, and how does it sound.

In discussing "truly" revived synthpop, there are no greater figures than the likes of Kavinsky. Kavinsky is a French producer, who claims to have started making music on an old Apple PC, before moving on to a MX-7, a more familiar piece of equipment from the eighties. His musical career didn't start over night, instead hitting him in his late twenties. After many years as an actor, he was prompted by a few others in his own personal circle to start making and producing music, that they would then use in their own films. As such, his work is meant to be played with film; he, himself, says that his style is derived from the "electropop" of eighties film soundtracks. As such, it is worth discussing what has been laid out here thus far. First, is the hybridization of various artistic types, film and music being closely interwoven, which is something that we see quite often in hip. Next, is the collection of past themes or ideas, in the form of old films, and bringing them to the forefront and making them new again. This has always been an element of hip, the ability to revive and regenerate things from beyond the grave and make them new; it happened in the Lost Generation, in Modernism, and so on and so forth. In using a stage name, Kavinsky has also developed a persona, claiming that Kavinsky is someone or something who is dead, a zombie, after perishing in an automobile accident in 1986. His reemergence has been to preserve or represent his time, despite the fact that it is past. Primarily, Kavinsky's music has been produced and sold alongside films, one of his tracks appearing in the phenomenal film *Drive*. "Nightcall" has been his most popular song, bar none. The beat is slow paced and structured, with two vocalists, a singular grating and gravelly voice, representing the now dead Kavinsky, both warning and gesturing the listener forward. "I'm giving you a nightcall, to tell you how I feel. I want to drive you through the night, and down the hills. I'm gonna tell you something you don't want to hear. I'm gonna show you where it's dark. But have no fear." This duality of emotion is, as established, very important to the genre, as this character speaks in a way that is both trite and uninspired, but the release of these emotions is legitimate; it feels authentic. In response to him, there is a clear and floating female vocalist, who resonates with him. "There's something inside you; it's hard to explain. They're talking about you, boy, but you're not the same." The subtle indication that the singer, and the listener somehow have changed is important to the existential themes of synthwave; this event has passed, and you've confronted it, and in doing so you are something of your own creation, something undead, maybe, but also something different entirely.

Darkwave is the grimy, little brother of all things synthwave. The distinct difference comes from the tone of the music as a whole; using the same sort of style and construction to build their music, they added dark and inward focused lyrics that would be underlined by a sense of sorrow. In addition, they took some cues from punk and metal in how they built their sound. Something nearly religious can be found in the pieces, be it an orchestral arrangement or an organ. Lastly, in terms of aesthetic, they rely on things that are typically paganistic or counter to the religion of the masses. Perturbator is a mainstay in this category.

Also French, Perturbator has his own mythos and ideology, drawing on the atmosphere and strengths of early-to-mid-eighties horror and sci-fi flicks. He frequently refers people to *Blade Runner* as his all-time favorite. In his own character, Perturbator is man, myth, and legend. His own set up is unknown, as he is something of an enigma himself. He does few live shows, but maintains a very active social media presence, answering questions from nearly anyone, at any time. In his past, he was the guitarist for a metal band, and the influence frequently shows in how he performs and in his opinion on music, which can occasionally be overwhelming and overhyped, while still absolutely soaked in darkness. Again, we see the hybrid connection between music and film, though this time, Perturbator focuses on some of the darker or harsher elements, preferring eighties films of an equally dark but exhilarating nature; horror films excite us, and his music seeks to do the same. In discussing his work, one of his seminal tracks would have to be "Minuit." In terms of composition, it lacks some of the harsher elements that his work is known for, ("Humans are Such Easy Prey" would be more fitting, perhaps) but it captures the more gothic, slow-paced and morose elements of his work. Additionally, it works with a science fiction theme of identity, and change. This song also features a pair of vocalists, again male and female, in a sort of call and response. "When I was a small child, obsessed with the future, I didn't believe in fate. I didn't believe in much of anything. Now that I'm a weathered machine, I'd give it all, I'd give everything, to have you here to believe, to believe in me." In a way, these lyrics are almost cheesy, like disgustingly so, but they are so heartfelt, and believed by the speaker that they still break through the facade. There is a gentleness to them, a pain. Additionally, the smoky vocals make it seem clearly digitized, but like he seeks his own organic past again; this conversion from human to robot is unnatural, as are singing robots. The response comes from a more human voice, though it is almost clustered in the synthesized sounds as well, almost drowned. Notably, she also sings in much shorter lines. "Who could ever hold, skin so cold? Hiding flesh and wire, only half awake. Doubting all the choices I make, feeling the heat but never the fire." The cover of the album depicts a half-clad woman (obviously a metal holdover) surrounded by a mechanical wasteland, with a pentagram front and center. In many ways, it feels like something organic or human is being contained in a mechanical form that it can't really escape or evade, and it only has some hold over, paganistic sentiment or something to worship in the creator, or in this case, Perturbator. This sort of artistic narcissism is entirely at home with hip, and even more, the unpopular or counter belief in something else, be it Zen or something paganistic, is also something quite hip. The sort of science fiction/cyberpunk conversion from human to android is also hip in how it considers how identity can be shifted, shaped or molded. This is a deeply existential theme in that regard, as well.

Chillwave is the relaxed, and summertime cousin of the genre, though it shares a direct stylistic route with the rest of synthpop. Frequently, it uses the same style of synthesized beats, with heavy sampling. There is a lot of filtering on the vocals, as well as layering, though the vocal scheme as a whole is simple and melodic. Typically, the music is more spatial, like a landscape of sound. The lyrics and tone are often dreamlike, and float on reflections. The instrumentation attempts to recreate the energy or human touch of the early eighties or late seventies. Usually, they are made up of small groups or a single person who composes near everything from a computer or laptop. The vocals are usually withdrawn, and not overwhelming. There is something simultaneously energetic and soothing about it. Often, drug references or ideas are inherent in the works, as are more progressive notions of sexuality; the ideas of partner swapping or smoking pot poolside come up frequently, though true love is appreciated and looked upon positively. Usually, it still ends badly, and almost insinuates that whomever is singing will probably hook up with a close friend of the beloved. Lastly, there is a sort of maintained independence or separation, despite what the situation may be.

Toro y Moi, stage name of Chaz Bundick, is a phrase taken from both French and Spanish, translating literally to "The Bull and Me." Despite the multilingual expression, Bundick is an American who began to produce music during the late years of his college career at the University of South Carolina, while studying graphic design. It is no surprise that he was closely associated with fellow chillwave artist, Ernest Greene, stage name, Washed Out. Further, the fact that Toro himself chooses and produces his own album art is something that ties back to the foundations of electropop as a genre. Again, we see hybridism in the art, much like O'Hara with the sculptors and painters of his era. Bundick's own proclivity for design somehow carries over into how his music is created and processed, and with great success. From Toro y Moi's own discography, few songs touch the same sort of topics as the aptly named "High Living," which is, conveniently and certainly coincidentally, four minutes and twenty seconds long. The song begins with smoky and simple instrumentation, with a faint shriek, as if to alert you to the fact that someone long missed has come to visit. Gentle key presses on the synthesizer seem to chortle in accordance with the vocals, as they elicit a sort of free and floating nature of their own as the singer declares more than a few things. "You and me, can be what we want to be. Don't you let this come falling down on me. I can hold it in my arms, and I don't expect anything in return. We'll be living high, living. We'll be getting up when we're down." These lines, despite their delivery, share a few various themes. The first is the sort of combination of people, the coupling of a pair, and their freedom to be something without a name or title. Whether this is meant to refer to their way of life or their sexual freedom is kind of up in the air. The second line is more of an indictment, asking whoever this woman is to make sure there isn't any fallout from whatever it is. If they are a couple, then she shouldn't intrude on him or limit him in any way. This shares a sort of ideology with the developed French existentialism, which insisted that one's only obligation was to oneself, and that anyone else had no right to infringe on that. The last lines underline a sense of community; he doesn't want any payment, not of the traditional type, and insists that his lifestyle is one of ascension, whether that means mental or emotional. It seems as if this all might be a facade, in the end, as they are just "getting up when" they're already down. The notion of freedom, sexual or in terms of identity, the reference to mind-altering drugs, and even the delivery of this whole scene is very hip, as we understand it. While it lacks some of the punch, it definitely fits the aesthetic and vibe.

Finally, vaporwave is the discordant, and nearly incomprehensible stepchild of synthpop. Almost a satire, but definitely a critique, vaporwave intends to parody consumer culture, or the society of money making, while using the avenue of New Age music in order to display things that are simultaneously nostalgic and outmoded. "Curious artifacts" come up quite a bit. In terms of frequent imagery, it makes use of glitch art, or computer edited photographs, in order to somehow breakdown or misrepresent a specific idea or set thereof. Classic sculpture appears quite often, as well as early Internet website design and badly constructed computer models, in order to represent concepts of various natures. The name comes from "vaporware" or announced products that are never manufactured or produced. The music itself degrades in quality, in an attempt to show the failing promises of standing economic or financial systems, or institutions in general.

Blank Banshee, as a musical group, is far more enigmatic than the others. The nature of their musical distribution is a free model; it's distributed online, in a free to download format, on a webpage. He is from British Columbia, and began to release music in 2012. In addition to being a musical artist, he is also a visual artist. Little is known about him, and he has been known to wear a mask while performing. He has only given one interview. In discussing his work, it is best to target the song, "Teen Pregnancy." Its delivery is airy and dynamic, while also extremely melodic and morose. It instills a deep and terrifying sense of pain, almost inciting its own form of nostalgia on the listener. "I'm just a kid. It was just a little mistake." These are the only lines of the song, and deliver a gut punch when thought of in the context of the work as a whole. The clever modification of the delivering voice helps alleviate the separation between the digitization of the music and the humanoid vocals. The cover of the album is also a rendering of a human face, though it lacks any hair and a torso. Its eyes are transparent and absent. (This was also made by the artist.) While the meaning of the work might be ambiguous, something about it is stirring. The utterance of the lines almost makes the piece seem like someone who has been caught in the candy jar, but will be punished for eternity. Additionally, this promotes the idea that somehow child rearing isn't okay; that reproduction isn't okay; that it is robbing someone of something, their childhood, and in a way, their humanity. A single mistake has ruined them. This idea of fatalism, as well as the loss of individuality in the face of traditional values, is very hip. It emphasizes the idea that if one simply concedes and conforms to traditional standards, then they become some strange face with no brain, no hair, or eyes. They become digitized, like the music, and our humanity becomes nostalgic or forgotten. The sampling of various beats constantly breaks the work up into a bunch of jagged and almost indigestible pieces, but there is something about them that flows, that reconstructs into one whole again, but it paints a picture we don't have to like.

In closing, synthpop and its subgenres are quite hip and touch on a variety of subjects across the board. Sentimentality, but also irony and deconstructionism are all interwoven, and that's the essence of hip. First, in synthpop revival, there is frequent imagery of being undead, or being revived, as well as existential undertones of being changed by a traumatic event. For darkwave, there is the promotion of sci-fi aesthetic, but the emphasis falls on something darker and more constructed around artistic narcissism, as well as the alteration of identity and loss of self, a deeply existential problem. Chillwave, despite its airy nature, focuses more on sexual liberation and the use of mind-altering drugs, and often deals with notions of self in conflict with the selves of others, and a seeming inability to mesh with other people on a more final level. Vaporwave is an anti-consumerist musical construction, which focuses more on satirizing the existing power structure in order to make a point, or emphasize a point of ridicule, but also offers one of the more starkly emotional pieces amongst the genre. Each part of the genre also emphasizes a hybridity in their work, be it film and music, or visual art and music. This, too, is quite hip, as it shows a multi-faceted construction of the world as a whole.

Lexington Community Gardens

Monica Alden, Kate Heinonen, Weston Owen, Esther Putman, and Samuel Wycoff

Throughout the semester they continually worked hard to interrogate the relationships between local Lexington food spaces and food culture, rhetoric, and larger national and global issues relating to food. The product of this hard work and research is their Group Wiki which is a user-friendly, aesthetically pleasing, thorough exploration of Community Gardens in the Lexington area. I look forward to seeing what these students produce as they continue on with their academic careers, and I am proud to have been able to work with them last semester.

—Deirdre Mikolajcik

Scan the QR code to see the project online.

Mental Health

Justin Bunch, Josh Carroll, Kaylee Lloyd, Katy Baxter, and Julien Thibault

In my mind, this group created such a great podcast from two fundamental ingredients: responsibility and discipline. Sure, we went over good techniques for composing podcasts in class, and they utilized those techniques. Sure, we talked about good oral delivery, and they used their voices to good effect. But the two ingredients that I mentioned earlier—responsibility and discipline—gave the podcast another dimension. So let me briefly outline those ingredients.

The group's podcast is about mental health issues as they play out for college students. This is an important topic that universities are becoming more aware of, and it is a topic that some of the group has personal experience with. Justin, Josh, Kaylee, Katy, and Julien cared about this topic. Out of this care came a sense of responsibility, a need to use their compositional acumen to help others.

But care is not always enough to create a work that will connect with others in important ways. This is where discipline is essential. Discipline keeps us engaged with the things we care about. Discipline commits us to making our writing—and our world—better. Little by little, person by person.

—Beth Connors-Manke

Scan the QR code to see the project online.

Gato del Sol

Parker Householder, Hayley McCole, Lisa Nguyen, Fiorella Riveros Salazar, and Andrew Thomas

I think it's safe to say that both instructors and students approach group work with a certain level of dread, a dread which is not always unwarranted. Even when each member of the group is a high achiever, sometimes the clash of personalities gets in the way. This group, however, is the veritable dream team of group work. They balanced strong personalities, committed to open dialogue, worked really hard, and in the end created an incredibly professional piece that contributes to the UK community. From Parker's attention to detail, Hayley's tireless dedication, Andrew's energetic imagination, Lisa's polished creativity, to Fio's CEO-like powers of organization, I could not be prouder of them and can't wait to see how they keep changing the world for good.

—Anna Stone

Scan the QR code to see the project online.

Consumers Against Corporations

Ally Iglesias, Micah Finley, Dean Crockett, and Logan Skeens

Ally, Micah, Dean, and Logan's group documentary reveals an uncomfortable truth that most of the American public is comfortable ignoring: we don't actually know what we are buying. Their investigative documentary highlights how we, as consumers, are constantly bombarded with false—or extremely confusing and contradictory information—that prevents many people from understanding what their money is *actually* being spent on and what corporation reaps the profits. They reveal how often one corporation owns multiple companies that advertise and sell products by using conflicting messages. And so we must ask … do we really know what messages, beliefs, or causes our money supports? Do we even know what corporation is responsible for the products we buy? Are we as aware of our consumerist actions as we think we are? With a combination of delightful humor, facts, compelling information, impressive graphics, and animation, this group's documentary forces us to confront a rarely discussed truth about consumerism and advertising. Ally, Micah, Dean, and Logan taught me more than I'd ever expect to know about this topic, and even though I'm still slightly bitter about how they've impacted my shopping habits, I'm incredibly proud of them and the hard work they put into this project.

—Cate Gooch

Scan the QR code to see the project online.

Kentucky Farm Chain

Sara Newman, Maygen Semall, and Carmen Siguenza

Teaching Business and Technical Writing, I rarely get to see innovative projects at the end of the semester. The nature of these courses makes it all the more impressive and rewarding when students do produce work that is both creative and socially conscious. Sara Newman, Maygen Semall, and Carmen Siguenza have done just this with their website for the Kentucky Farm Chain, a community supported agriculture, or CSA, initiative in central Kentucky designed to inform individuals about and engage them with local farms and food movements. The website is sleekly designed, thoroughly informative, and socially relevant. Please join me in congratulating Sara, Maygen, and Carmen for their accomplishment.

—Alex Menrisky

Scan the QR code to see the project online.